HYGGE

An Introduction to the Danish Art of Cozy Living

© Copyright 2017 by Amy White and Ryan James - All rights reserved.

The following Book is reproduced below with the goal of providing information that is as accurate and as reliable as possible. Regardless, purchasing this Book can be seen as consent to the fact that both the publisher and the author of this book are in no way experts on the topics discussed within, and that any recommendations or suggestions made herein are for entertainment purposes only. Professionals should be consulted as needed before undertaking any of the action endorsed herein.

This declaration is deemed fair and valid by both the American Bar Association and the Committee of Publishers Association and is legally binding throughout the United States.

Furthermore, the transmission, duplication or reproduction of any of the following work, including precise information, will be considered an illegal act, irrespective whether it is done electronically or in print. The legality extends to creating a secondary or tertiary copy of the work or a recorded copy and is only allowed with express written consent of the Publisher. All additional rights are reserved.

The information in the following pages is broadly considered to be a truthful and accurate account of facts, and as such any inattention, use or misuse of the information in question by the reader will render any resulting actions solely under their purview. There are no scenarios in which the publisher or the original author of this work can be in any fashion deemed liable for any hardship or damages that may befall them after undertaking information described herein.

Additionally, the information found on the following pages is intended for informational purposes only and should thus be considered, universal. As befitting its nature, the information presented is without assurance regarding its continued validity or interim quality. Trademarks that mentioned are done without written consent and can in no way be considered an endorsement from the trademark holder.

Table of Contents

Introduction 1

Chapter 1: What is Hygge and How Did It Evolve? 4

Chapter 2: Hygge and Happiness................................11

Chapter 3: Tips on How to Make Your Home More Hygge..20

Chapter 4: Prioritizing the People in Your Life Properly 29

Chapter 5: Finding the Food and Hygge Balance........36

Chapter 6: Indulging and Investing in Yourself 46

Chapter 7: Activities with Friends that Are So Hygge it Hurts 56

Chapter 8: Hygge Fashion Tips that Will Make Your Wardrobe Pop..64

Conclusion..71

INTRODUCTION

Congratulations on purchasing your personal copy of *Hygge: An Introduction to the Danish Art of Cozy Living*. Thank you for doing so.

The following chapters will discuss the Danish lifestyle trend that is known as hygge. Perhaps you've heard of hygge before, and want to learn more about it, or perhaps you know nothing about hygge but are excited to learn about how this easygoing mindset and way of life can influence how you live for the better. Either way, the ideas that will be presented in this book are sure to be useful to you in a way that will lead to less stress and more pleasure on a daily basis. As our lives become busier and busier through new developments in technology, it's nice to know that it's still possible to live in a way that promotes togetherness, coziness, and long-term happiness. These concepts are what hygge is all about, and these are the types of nuanced pleasures that hygge can offer your life.

The last chapter is going to discuss how you can create a hygge-optimized fashion sense for you and your closet. The concepts that are going to be presented in this book can be used during any time of the year, and this is similar to some of the other topics that will be discussed in this book. Hygge can infiltrate many aspects of your life, including the activities that you do, the clothes that you wear, the food that you eat, and the mindset that you have about life in general. As you're going to find, hygge is as much about how you design the interior of your home and how you dress yourself as it is about cultivating positive relationships that will leave you and your loved ones feeling supported and happy on a consistent basis.

There are plenty of books on this subject on the market, thanks again for choosing this one! Every effort was made to ensure it is full of as much useful information as possible. Please enjoy!

Congratulations on getting your personal copy of *Hygge: An Introduction to the Danish Art of Cozy Living*.

Enjoy the rest of this book!

CHAPTER 1

WHAT IS HYGGE AND HOW DID IT EVOLVE?

Dieting trends seem to always seem to be changing, and it can sometimes be difficult to keep up with the latest dieting fad. Just a few dieting trends include the Atkins Diet, the South Beach Diet, the Wheat Belly Diet, and Jenny Craig. The list goes on, yet the certainty that these diets do in fact work over the long-term is something that can be debated, given the fact that there are so many different diets out there. On the other hand, dieting for the mind is discussed much less than is physical dieting for the body. Finding a balance between the stress that comes with living in the modern technological age and relaxation is often not discussed. Instead, people will typically either become prescribed to medication that will relax them with side effects, or they will simply push through the stress that they feel until they become stress eaters, have a heart attack, or worse. None of these outcomes seem ideal to me.

Hygge As the Answer to Stress Alleviation

Instead of forcing yourself to adapt to the stressful lifestyle that is being pressed upon you by society, another option that you have is to resist it through alternative living techniques. This is where hygge comes into play. Hygge, in the most basic sense, can be defined as the Danish word for a feeling of contentment and comfort. You will see most translations define hygge as being the Danish word for "cozy", but it's important to note that no literal translation actually exists between the two words. Mostly deriving from the Netherlands, many people claim that hygge is what largely contributes to Denmark competing with places like Iceland and Switzerland as being home to the happiest people on earth.

One of the biggest reasons why the notion of hygge is important to the people of Denmark is because of their exceptionally long winters. Denmark is known for going through periods of up to seventeen hours of darkness per day during the winter, and this darkness brings with it temperatures that are well below zero degrees. These two weather conditions would cause you to initially think that people who live in this type of environment would become incredibly unhappy or even suicidal. Instead, Denmark's reliance on the hygge allows its population to remain entertained, content and happy during even the darkest months of the season.

Comfort Rather than Deprivation

When thinking about how the civilians of Denmark are forced to live in isolation and darkness for months at a time, it's safe to say that they are in a sense isolated from the traditional luxuries that someone who lives in a more temperate area is. For this reason, Danish people as a whole are much less likely to indulge in the types of deprivation techniques that people from both the United States and the United Kingdom are more prone to using. For example, studies have shown that there are far less fad dieters in Denmark than there are in both America and the UK.

Because of the fact that Denmark does suffer from a colder climate throughout the year, people are more focused on making the best of the situation, rather than depriving themselves of anything more than is necessary. From the tendencies that are evident from the behavior of the average Danish person, it's easy to see that a key element of living hygge involves being kind to oneself all of the time. By replacing deprivation with exhibiting kindness to oneself and to others, hygge allows the Danes to feel a greater sense of contentment with their lives, regardless of the specific circumstances in which they find themselves.

The Hygge Lingo

Now that you have a better understanding of how hygge came to be and what this lifestyle values, we will get into how you can pronounce this word properly. You might be thinking that the word hygge is pronounced "Hig-gee", but that is not the case. Instead, if you're looking to pronounce this word properly, you're going to pronounce it "hue-guh". Don't worry, if this pronunciation does not seem all that natural to you, you likely won't be faulted for pronouncing it as it comes naturally to you. In fact, if someone were to challenge your pronunciation of this word, you could simply remind them that you're most comfortable pronouncing it your own way, and in doing so you are completely upholding hygge principles.

Without getting too technical into the Danish language, another term that is sometimes used alongside of the word hygge is the word "hyggeligt". This is an adjective that Danish people use after they've enjoyed time in someone else's home. Even if you don't think that you're ever going to find yourself in a situation where using the term hyggeligt would be appropriate, it is still interesting to see how the term hygge can be used to describe multiple types of comfort in Denmark. The term hyggeligt makes it apparent that the term hygge can expand to include situations where you're comfy with other people. In this way, hygge as a concept is able to abstractly influence your relationships with others in a positive manner. By recognizing that an important part of hygge involves comradery with the people around you, it's possible to see how hygge has become a phenomenon within the Danish community. It doesn't matter what your social status is in Denmark or how much money you make. Everyone within their society is influenced by the principles of hygge, one way or another.

It's the Little Things

As you're going to find after reading the rest of what this book has to offer, a hygge lifestyle emphasizes small, rather than large, gestures. For example, a small act that would be considered hygge in nature would be to sit on your back porch during a cold winter evening, while sipping hot cocoa from a mug that was handmade by a loved one while wearing wool mittens and an extremely warm jacket. Due to the fact that the Danes are the ones who coined the hygge trend, a lot of the imagery surrounding this style emphasizes being in a colder climate; however, if you're looking to expand the definition of hygge to include your particular locale, there's no reason why the coziness that is inherent to hygge necessarily has to mean that you're bundled up in a cold environment.

CHAPTER 2

HYGGE AND HAPPINESS

Now that you know what hygge is and how to pronounce it (sort of), this next chapter is going to discuss how you can begin to cultivate the hygge mindset in a way that will generate long-term happiness. Of course, this book is going to discuss actions that you can take that will lead to the outward appearance that you're adapting to the hygge lifestyle; however, without internal recognition of this new way of life, it will be less likely that you'll ever truly adapt to what hygge is all about. Hygge starts in the heart, and that's what this will chapter will discuss, how you can begin to cultivate hygge principles within yourself prior to developing an outwardly hygge lifestyle.

Rethinking the Notion of Perfection

One of the first steps that you can take towards truly understanding what hygge can offer your life is to resist the urge to think in terms of perfection. In a modern Westernized society, it can sometimes seem as if we are constantly pushing ourselves to constantly be better than we already are. While of course, progress can certainly be a positive, it's also possible to surpass a point of where constant progress is attainable. For example, emphasis on body image in the United States has manifested itself into many people becoming fitness-crazed. Additionally, plastic surgery rates have continued to rise all around the world. While the United States is not the first country in terms of the highest plastic surgery rates, it still does rank rather high, coming in sixth out of all the countries in the world. The country where plastic surgery is the most popular is South Korea, followed by Greece, Italy, and Brazil.

It's important to note that there has been a recent rise in plastic surgery in Denmark, but these rates still pale in comparison to the increase in plastic surgery rates in other parts of the world. This increasingly prevalent tendency for women in particular to think that "perfection" is possible from the perspective of their physique is an indication that many societies are caught up in obtaining some type of perfection for themselves. Through hygge, Denmark is able to somewhat set themselves apart from the global phenomenon of perfection that is occurring. The next question that you may have is how exactly is hygge facilitating this type of mindset?

Hygge as an Entry Point for More Self-Indulgence

Instead of focusing on perfection and how to best obtain it, someone who is mindfully involved in cultivating more hygge into his or her life is going to do so by being more self-indulgent. Instead of looking to abstain from the worldly pleasures of life, someone who is wrapped up in becoming more hygge is going to focus inward and take note of what it is that makes them feel cozy, at home, and safe. What this means is that instead of focusing on what is the "norm" in regards to any specific situation, you are instead focusing on how you could feel the most comfortable when a particular situation arises. Let's take a look at some of the ways that you can begin to concretely develop a more self-indulgent mindset for yourself, so that you stop thinking in terms of what is "right" and start thinking more in terms of what's "right for you".

Practice Gratitude Every Day

One of the closest concepts to hygge is gratitude. When you practice gratitude, you're able to appreciate the everyday things in life, rather than only feeling grateful when you're taking a big trip or coming into a lot of money. Cultivating gratitude involves pausing to recognize the world's countless nuances that are both incredibly beautiful as well as special. When you learn to bring more gratitude into your life, you're going to be able to not only become happier, but also become less materialistic. When someone is materialistic, it means that this person is likely going to try and find happiness through the items that he or she purchases.

This could be as simple as finding happiness in buying new clothes, but it could also be as expensive as buying a new car. The problem with finding happiness in things rather than through gratitude is that the newness of a material possession is going to erode over time. This means that if your happiness is linked to this material possession, your happiness is likely going to be temporary as well. This is why finding gratitude for what you have is important. As it relates to hygge, finding coziness within the smaller things in life goes completely hand-in-hand with being able to fully appreciate those smaller things. In this way, it should be easy to see that if you're simply going through the motions of becoming more hygge without taking the time to learn how to self-indulge, there's a good chance that you're never going to truly "get" it. Below are a few ways that you can start to practice gratitude, if you think that this is an area of your life that could use some work:

1. Note 5 Things You're Thankful for Each Day

A great way to jumpstart finding more gratitude in your life involves noting five things that you're thankful for each day. You can jot these five things down in some sort of gratitude journal, but you don't even have to do that! By simply going over five things in your head for which you're thankful each day, you're going to slowly train your brain to be able to pick out the small things that can be make you happier each day, which will lead to greater happiness over time.

2. Volunteer

Another way to appreciate what you have is to volunteer for organizations that are dedicated to helping people who have less than you do. By showing up for these people and providing them with your time, you'll likely be able to truly feel appreciative of all of the goodness that is in your own life.

3. Avoid Negative Media

The rise of the internet has made it possible to access countless media sources in a matter of seconds. Not only that, sensationalizing the news has almost become the norm rather than the exception. Gruesome details regarding terrible acts of violence, theft and other types of misdemeanors are literally at our fingertips. Whether or not you're aware of it, these types of details can weigh on the brain and provide you with a sense of pessimism over time. One way to keep the brain more positive is to simply avoid indulging in negative news stories when it's possible.

Indulge in Greater Self-Care

In addition to finding more gratitude in daily life, another way that the Danes use hygge methodology in a way that leads to more happiness is by focusing on self-care. Self-care involves participating in daily life more mindfully and less habitually. A great way that you can begin to become acquainted with the notion of self-care is to create a self-care kit for yourself. For example, this may mean that instead of coming home from work and plopping yourself down on the couch for hours on end, you instead prepare a self-care kit for yourself in advance. This kit may contain things such as warm socks, chocolates, a good book, and maybe even candles. By refocusing your energy on how you can relax properly instead of how you can zone out by watching mindless television, you'll likely find greater pleasure after you come home from a long day of work or school.

Less is More

Lastly, it's important to note that minimalism also has to do with hygge. While minimalism in itself is a separate philosophy from hygge, the two do interact somewhat. For example, hygge advocates for simplicity in your most intimate spaces, rather than a cluttered or unorganized environment. If you feel like you *need* everything in your environment right now, try to look at the concept of simplicity a different way. First, think about what your goals are in terms of how you want to obtain lasting happiness for yourself. In other words, what do you need in order to be happy? Start with this question, and try to seek out only the essentials, rather than the excess. By simply asking yourself this question, you'll be amazed at what you're able to find out about yourself.

CHAPTER 3

TIPS ON HOW TO MAKE YOUR HOME MORE HYGGE

Now that you have an understanding of how you can begin to cultivate a mindset that is largely hygge in nature, we will now turn our attention towards how you can go about turning your most intimate personal spaces into hygge-rich environments. This chapter is going to discuss hygge home decorating trends. After reading this chapter, you will have a perfect understanding the types of interior design techniques that you can bring into your home in order to provide your home with a comfier and all around cozier feeling. Let's take a look at how you can make your home hygge in ways that are as easy to implement as they are incredibly cozy and relaxing.

Interior Styling Tip 1: Light Your Home Appropriately

Both candles and fireplaces can be defined as two key aspects of the hygge lighting aesthetic. Candles are a huge aesthetic aspect of designing a hygge space. Even if you do not own a fireplace, thinking about how you can create lighting in your home in a way that connotes a feeling of warmness and glowing quality is a great way to start creating more of a hyggelig environment (hyggelig is an adjective form of the word hygge). If you're looking to make the lighting in your home more hygge, you should be looking to obtain a golden hue in your space. This type of color is usually naturally derived from the light that candles and fireplaces are able to contribute to a room. Types of artificial light that can bring more of a golden color to a room include the light that comes from vintage bulbs as well as light bulbs that are a lower wattage than a 100-watt bulb.

It's important to understand that while golden light is going to produce an all-around cozier feeling, there are some other advantages that also exist when you're able to introduce more golden lighting into your environment. For example, from a psychological perspective it's known that dimmer lighting can cause people to be in a better mood than they otherwise would be under normal lighting conditions. Additionally, people are usually better to communicate when the lighting is warmer and it's been also proven that they're able to think in a more creative capacity. Lastly, there has been some research done that suggests that when you spend time gazing at a fire, what you're essentially doing is relaxing your mind. All of these factors combine to produce the enhanced cozy feeling that hygge advocates.

Interior Styling Tip 2: Make Yourself a "Hyggekrog"

Another interior design look to consider that will nicely coincide with your desire to be more hygge involves creating what's known as a hyggekrog. In English, a hyggekrog would probably best be defined as a nook or some other type of relaxing space where you can unwind. Ideally, a hyggekrog is going to be located near a window, and will include cushions on the seats of the nook as well. Additionally, this nook space may be surrounded by bookcases, and may even be a place where you house a throw pillow or two and a blanket for your enjoyment. Finish off this space with a small table that can house some hearty snacks while you read or gaze out the window, and you'll be good to go. It's important to note that having a window for your hyggekrog is not essential. If you don't have a good window where you could set up this type of cozy environment for yourself, you can still create one from the layout that feels most appropriate for your individual space.

Interior Styling Tip 3: Make Your Bed a Lounger's Paradise

On the weekends, do you ever have the days when you feel like you don't want to get out of bed? For someone who is trying to make their space more hygge, he or she is going to want to make sure that their bed is fully equipped to handle the types of days when getting out of bed seems like an impossibility. The key ingredient to creating a cozier bed is to think layers. Especially if you live in a particularly cold region of the world, layers are going to make you feel not only warmer but also cozier due to the added weight that is going to be placed on the body.

Additionally, another important aspect of proper hygge bed etiquette involves making sure that you have the proper pillows. Unless you're someone who pays little attention to the finer things in life, you probably have an idea of the type of pillow that you prefer. Do you enjoy fluffy pillows that allow your head to melt into them, or do you prefer a pillow that is going to provide your head with some stiffer stability? Whatever your preference is, make sure that you have ample pillows available that are of this particular style. Lastly, another good product that you may want to consider investing in is a breakfast tray. Who doesn't love breakfast in bed?

Interior Styling Tip 4: The More Natural, the Better

Another facet of the hygge design culture involves natural elements being introduced into the home space. Specifically, the types of materials that hygge enthusiasts will tend to bring indoors include the elements of leather, wool, wood, and brick. When you introduce these elements into a space, the goal should be to create an aesthetic that is neutral and will make you feel calm while looking at it. Additionally, if you are thinking about introducing natural elements to a room, you should consider only implementing a couple of them so as not to bombard the space with contrast.

Interior Style Tip 5: Integrate Patterns or Texture

It's important that you keep the elements of the previous tip rather neutral in color and texture, because in addition to bringing natural elements into a space, another hygge tendency is to contrast this neutrality with specific textures or designs. For someone who lives in Denmark, the reality is that a lot of their winter months are going to be spent indoors. Without textures or patterns in their home that will bring some life into the space which they inhabit, their spaces would likely seem too boring over a long period of time cooped up in their home. For example, a hygge home may contain many wood elements, but may also contain one or two walls that are adorned with wallpaper with colored pineapples or fanciful animals on them. To this extent, the goal of the hygge home is to portray a feeling of both ease and playfulness simultaneously. Who ever said that playfulness could not also be relaxing?

Free Versus Expensive and Perfection through Décor

First of all, one of the key aspects of hygge design tactics that is important to understand is that you should be avoiding a completely manicured or uniform home. For example, in a hygge household this means that not all of the pillows in the living room area *must* match. Instead, perhaps your throw pillows are all different and have been chosen based on the fact that they all provide you with pleasure when you either look at them or lay on them in one way or another. While mixing and matching is okay when you're adopting hygge decorating ideals, this does not mean that free stuff is always the way to go. Remember, in addition to being cozy, hygge design is also simplistic. If you find that you're accumulating a bunch of free stuff that you're not using in an efficient manner, it's best to get rid of it. To this end, it's also important to keep in mind that free is not always the best thing regarding your decor. For someone who is looking to be more hygge, you want the coziest and most personally memorable goods filling up your home. On the other hand, being hygge doesn't have to cost a fortune either. Find your own personal balance.

Additionally, hygge is not at all about having the "perfect" space. When you are first starting to decorate, it's easy to get caught up in having good symmetry and balance throughout your home. For hygge design, a reliance on balance and symmetry is being replaced by the importance of your personal comfort. If things in your home don't match up perfectly, that's okay. The hygge lifestyle is more concerned about how you can create an environment where you will be able to feel most at home, regardless of how this environment compares to other types of homes in terms of "normalcy". This notion should excite you, because it asks you to be creative when it comes to truly making a space your own in a way that truly works for you.

CHAPTER 4

PRIORITIZING THE PEOPLE IN YOUR LIFE PROPERLY

What good would your hygge-decorated home be if you never had people over to entertain? A big part of the hygge way of life, in addition to being about decorating in a comfy way, also involves interacting with friends and family in a particular way. When life is busy, sometimes it can seem like we don't have much time for the people who are most important to us; however, when you start to live with hygge in mind, you may be surprised to find that suddenly you feel more mindful about prioritizing the people in your life. This chapter is going to discuss ways that you can begin to form relationships that are more hygge and less sterile or basic in nature.

Invite More People into Your Space

Once you have a home that is cozy and speaks perfectly to your personal ideals of comfort, why not share these ideals with others? If you live somewhere in the West, or in the United States, then there's a chance that you often resist the urge to invite others into your home on a regular basis. When you've created a cozy and inviting atmosphere, there should be nothing stopping you from bringing more people whom you care about spending time with into your home. While it may be initially daunting to think about having someone casually occupy your home for a long period of time, it's these types of casual interactions that will make you closer to someone. When you do end up inviting people into your hygge home, try to resist the urge to have an "agenda". Instead, simply allow things to unfold as they may.

Lurk More!

Another concept that is unique to hygge when it comes to developing better and more mindful relationships with the people around you are the idea of lurking more. This goes hand-in-hand with not setting an agenda when you invite someone over into your home. Rather than conversing with someone only to make a point or so that you can obtain the information that you need, a better approach might be to stick around after you've gotten the information that you're seeking and see how else you can connect with the person to whom you're talking. This will allow you to perhaps find out more about the person that would otherwise not be possible if you were to simply stop talking to the person after figuring out the information that you need. Another benefit of lurking is that it often allows you to better understand where the other person is coming from as well as their perspective on life. This is a humbling and simultaneously unifying experience that most Danes are good at cultivating.

Think "Hang Out" Instead of Formal Wine and Dine

Another important aspect of interacting with people in a more hygge fashion is to think about the types of gatherings you want to have. The type of gathering that you should be trying to have if you're keeping within hygge ideals should be one that is informal, casual, and cozy. For example, instead of inviting your friends over for a dinner party that will include a three-course meal of salad, entrée and dessert with copious amounts of wine, it might be a better idea to host a dinner that will include large casseroles of comfort food, beer, and any other types of libations that you know your guests love. From the perspective of hygge, there's no real point in serving food that people are not going to absolutely love. The way that you present the meal is going to have a big impact on how formal the event feels. It's important to keep this in mind as you move through the dinner planning process.

Initiate a Bonfire Hang

A bonfire can be considered to be the perfect hygge setting. Even if you don't have a bonfire of your own or know how to make one from scratch, these days it's incredibly easy to find a chimenea or outdoor fireplace at a home improvement store for a relatively cheap price. Bonfires, with their emphasis on both fire and natural elements that are used to start them, are quite hygge in nature. Additionally, a bonfire is also a casual setting that will allow you to talk intimately with your friends with few interruptions. If you don't personally own a bonfire and don't plan on purchasing one anytime soon, there might be places within the vicinity in which you live that has a bonfire that you can go to instead. Of course, these types of places are likely going to be more crowded than if you were sitting around your own personal bonfire, so you have to decide if this type of outing is worth it to you.

Perform Loving Actions

Living more of a hygge lifestyle certainly does not mean that it's necessary to be constantly inviting people into your home in order to hang out. If you are a truly busy person and don't have a lot of time to spare in terms of formally spending long periods of time with another person, you can still show the important people in your life that you care about them. Remember, friendships require upkeep in order to work, and this is why it's important to somewhat frequently reach out to the people you care about and show them how they mean a lot to you. This can be as simple as sending them an email or a handwritten letter, or it could be as complex as sending them a gift through the mail. Remember, hygge is all about the little things, which is why this type of gesture can go a long way from a friend point of view.

Start a New Hygge-Inspired Tradition

Another way that you can spend more time around the people whom you care about and create new memories at the same time involves starting a new tradition. The word "tradition" can be a bit misleading, because it is usually used when discussing holidays or special events. In reality, a tradition can be as simple as hosting a monthly game night at your house, or planning an activity that you and your friends are going to participate in once a year. In this way, you are planning for a good time in the future, which can often keep the people in your life excited and eager to spend time with you and your closest pals. By creating something that is "special", you're essentially making it more likely that the people with whom you're closest are going to be around now and far into the future.

CHAPTER 5

FINDING THE FOOD AND HYGGE BALANCE

By now, you should be able to see that there are hygge ideals that can be obtained for almost any aspect of your life, including food. This chapter is going to focus on the types of foods that you can enjoy that will certainly leave you feeling cozy, satisfied, and happy. After reading this chapter, not only will you have a better understanding of the types of foods that you should be consuming in order to feel hygge yourself; you'll also have developed a strong knowledge of how to interact with food in a way that will leave the people around you feeling loved and happy as well.

Making It Yourself Versus Buying It in the Store

One of the first important points to recognize about food in a hygge home is that a lot of the food that is consumed should be food that has been prepared by you or by someone with whom you live. Yes, baking hearty goods for your entire household often takes a lot of time, but the goal when you're cooking hygge food is to make it mindfully, so that the person who is consuming it is able to taste the love and effort that you've put into it in every bite. From the perspective of hygge, it's not considered lazy to purchase goods in the store; obviously, some food is better off being bought rather than made yourself. A big reason why the hygge foods that we're going to discuss should be made from scratch, when possible, is because of the delicious smells that these foods can bring into your home. Similar to the cozy feeling you can get when cookies are baking in the oven, hygge definitely advocates for cooking and baking foods that will leave your house smelling hearty and wonderful.

Foods that Are Considered Hygge

Now that you know what the major benefits are in terms of cooking and baking your own hygge food, now it is time to look at some of the specific types of foods that you can make if you want to embody hygge ideals in the kitchen. Remember, hygge is about mindfulness. This means that even if you end up botching the recipe that you're working on, it's important to find content in the actual process of making the food in question. If you can't find personal enjoyment in the activity itself, you're not deriving the hygge essence from the activity in question. Let's take a look at some of the most popular hygge foods so that you can get them into your kitchen as quickly as possible.

Hygge Food 1: Cinnamon Buns

If you've ever gone to a bakery or even a Dunkin Donuts to purchase a donut or a muffin with your coffee in the morning, then you already know how purchasing this type of treat can feel. When you make cinnamon buns at home, this feeling is enhanced because you've made these delicacies yourself. Even if you made your cinnamon buns ahead of time and reheat them for breakfast during the week, drinking your morning coffee with a homemade cinnamon bun in hand will likely relax you and provide you with a great start to your morning.

Hygge Food 2: Smorrebrod

You don't have to use these Danish terms in your own everyday language, but they're fun to try to pronounce nonetheless! Smorrebrod can loosely be translated to mean "stuff on toast". Remember, being hygge is certainly not about finding perfection in your life, but it is about having a certain level of simplicity to it. We don't always have the perfect ingredients in the home. Sometimes, we have to work with what we've got. That's what the notion of smorrebrod is all about. Avocado, hard boiled eggs, cream cheese, and even your favorite sliced up vegetables are all great ways that you can spice up a piece of boring old toast.

Hygge Food 3: Swedish Meatballs

If you have ever gone shopping at Ikea, then you should already know that a key feature of any Ikea outing involves dining at their cafeteria and indulging in some Swedish meatballs after a long day of furniture shopping. These types of meatballs offer a sweeter flavor than a regular Italian meatball, and can easily be consumed with other hearty foods such as potatoes and gravy. My mouth is starting to water just thinking about how delicious this type of comfort food would be on a cloudy and cold evening.

Hygge Food 4: Stew or Chili

Another great comfort food that can be considered hygge in nature are stews and chilis. As long as you have a slow cooker or have room on your stove for a large pot to simmer for long hours on end, you're going to be able to experience the delicious smells that will emanate from a stew or chili dish. What's also great about this type of meal is that it can serve a lot of people and it is relatively easy to make and maintain. A stew or a chili could be the perfect dinner to make while you're hosting a game night or another type of casual gathering at your house. This way, there will be pleasant aromas wafting through your house all evening, and you won't have all that much actual cooking to do.

Hygge Food 5: Soup

Making a hearty soup for yourself and for your loved ones is extremely hygge in nature. There's nothing like a warm and indulgent soup to eat while you're curled up on the couch watching a movie with a friend or a significant other. It's important to note here that some soups are better than others. The best advice is to start simple if you've never made soup before. For example, I know someone who had little experience with cooking soup, but he wanted to try it. He decided to try and make celery root soup, and it turned out to be a disaster. He had never cooked with celery root before, and the flavor of the soup ended up being metallic, too acidic, and to put it bluntly awful. Some easy soups that you should try to make prior to making anything complicated include tomato soup, potato and corn chowder, or butternut squash soup with bacon.

Hygge Food Type 6: Bread

Another major food group that is a part of any serious hygge diet is bread. Cooking bread inside of your home is going to produce a lovely aroma that is unmatched in terms of coziness. Additionally, another great hygge idea that you can use for your own indulgency involves making your own soup and your own bread at the same time. Of course, the amount of work that this type of cooking endeavor requires should not be taken lightly. Bread in particular can be rather difficult to make, especially if you are not using a bread kit and are instead looking to completely make this bread from scratch. In order to make bread, you are going to need to possess a lot of patience, because bread can easily go from appearing to be rising nicely to looking like a pancake or a wafer. Take your time, and understand that bread making requires great attention to detail and accuracy. This will allow you to make bread while starting on the right foot.

Hygge Food Type 7: Eat More Porridge

Porridge is a word that you don't often hear if you live in the United States; however, for a Danish person, porridge could almost be considered to be a staple food of their diet. Oatmeal is quite similar to porridge, but it's important to understand that oatmeal is often defined as a *type* of porridge that exists within the porridge family. While oatmeal is almost always made with some type of grain, porridge can be made with vegetables or even legumes in some cases. Porridge is a comfort food in the sense that it is almost always served hot, and there are many varieties of porridge that you can consume. In this way, it's safe to say that porridge is similar to the smorrebrod that we've already discussed. If you're creative, you should be able to concoct a porridge meal from simple and diverse ingredients in your home.

Hygge Foods and Your Diet

Even though hygge is all about being indulgent, cozy and eating comfort food, it's important to note that this does not mean that you should go insane with the amount of comfort food that you're eating on a daily basis. As with any diet, variety is important, especially from a health perspective. Of course, we are all probably excited about the fact that a major part of the hygge diet seems to revolve around bread; however, this does not mean that this book is advocating for daily consumption of many slices of bread. In fact, hygge is as much as mindfulness as it is about indulgence and comfort.

It's unlikely that you feel comfortable in your own body if you're plumping yourself up by consuming comfort foods on a daily basis. When your health is on the line, it's crucial that you understand your own body's limits, so that you don't end up getting fat or sick. It's that simple. The bottom line is, use your discretion when cooking and consuming heavy levels of carbohydrates and comfort food.

CHAPTER 6

INDULGING AND INVESTING IN YOURSELF

Now that you know what types of food you should be cooking when you want to be hygge, this next chapter is going to focus on the types of activities you can do in order to enjoy these foods while you hygge out. Remember, one of the major reasons why the Danes are so good at entertaining themselves through simple pleasures is because they spend a lot of their time in darkness during the winter months. For this reason, self-entertainment is almost essential for someone who is living in Denmark. The result of this need for self-entertainment is happiness, because the Danes are able to find and derive pleasure from hobbies that may be considered "boring" to someone who is constantly finding new avenues for entertainment. The hobbies listed in this chapter are important because once you start to learn how to entertain yourself and feel pleasure in spending some time alone, happiness should be quite easy to obtain.

Additionally, there is sometimes a tendency in Western society to be constantly "doing" something. You may find that when you're alone and have nothing to do, you're suddenly bored or uninterested in life. This is perhaps the wrong way to be living. If you can slowly start to spend longer amounts of time by yourself, doing an activity that is personally pleasing to you, you may find that you're suddenly finding out new things about yourself that you previously did not know or understand. Spending time alone can be therapeutic, yet people in Western society often shy away from it. Perhaps this is because spending time alone won't look fabulous in a social media photo, or because there are so many sources of entertainment these days that it can sometimes seem pointless to do anything by yourself. To make this more concrete, below is a list of benefits that come with spending time alone:

1. **Increases Productivity:** Spending time alone allows you to relax and truly be yourself in a way that is arguably not possible, even when the person who is around is someone who you trust and love. By taking time out of your day to spend time alone and regroup, you're allowing the brain to recharge and prepare for the next time it has to work and be productive.

2. **Establishes Your Voice:** Have you ever been around a friend who is particularly domineering? Whenever you're in a group setting, you're opening yourself up to being coerced into thinking and making decisions based on whatever the group consensus is at the time. When you spend time alone, the truth of the matter is that you get to know yourself better

than you do when you're being influenced by other people. This is especially going to be true if you're someone who is typically shy or have a more "go with the flow" personality. Additionally, people often like people more who have their own opinion on things. In this way, spending more time alone will allow you to feel more confident when it comes time to making your first heard in social situations.

3. **Allows for More Effective Problem Solving:** Lastly, another reason why spending time alone can be cathartic is because it can help you to solve problems in a more effective manner. Whether it be the people around you who are trying to influence the way that you go about solving a problem, or it's the digital media that may be influencing you, the best way to solve a problem is often by thinking it through on your own. At the end of the day, you have to live with the decisions that you're making, so by spending time alone you're able to truly think

through any type of problem that you may be having.

Take Up Knitting or Crocheting

One hobby that will most likely allow you to feel relaxed, concentrated, and inspired all at the same time involves taking up knitting or crocheting. It can be argued that learning how to crochet is easier than learning how to knit, because crocheting only involves using one tool while knitting involves using two tools. This being the case, the best advice is to start taking up crocheting and then work towards learning how to knit. If you know someone who already understands how to do one of these hobbies, then you may want to reach out to him or her and see if they will agree to provide you with some pointers. Once you get the hang of either activity that you choose, you're likely going to enjoy the hobby because it will allow you to concentrate on the task at hand as well as easily see the progress that you're making over a short period of time. Even if you start simple, what one day will look like a piece of string will suddenly turn into a beautiful blanket or a scarf in no time at all.

Meditate

Another great way to truly find inner peace and contentment is through meditation. Meditation allows you to slow down, and can also help you to see things more objectively than they otherwise may seem. A great application that can help you get more into meditating is known as headspace. This application walks you through meditation by increasing the length of time that you spend meditating over the course of a week as well as guiding you through the meditation with a peaceful and soothing instructor. Everyone has five minutes that they can spend meditating, and meditation can be a great way to truly turn inward and slow down the busy thoughts that you may be having throughout the day. In this way, meditation is able to provide an individual with a tremendous amount of clarity and relaxation, especially after a particularly long or stressful day.

Read a Book Series

If you love to read and are looking to become more consistent in reading on a regular basis, you can challenge yourself to start reading a popular book series. When you read a book that is not in a series, you're able to fall in love with the characters, but once the book is over you can't get your fix of these characters and their particular plotlines anymore. This is where a book series differs from a single book that is written on its own. As long as the series is good, you'll likely want to read all of the books that are in it. Investing in a book series will help you to spend less time mindlessly watching television or binging on Netflix. Instead, you'll be able to spend time alone with your thoughts and with the characters in the book series as well.

Declutter

Perhaps you're someone who knows that clutter is one of your weaknesses. Your house is filled with stuff that you may need one day in the future, but that you haven't actually touched in a number of months or years. If you're a particularly unorganized person, there are still steps that you can take to declutter your home and your life little by little. For example, you could consider throwing out five things that you don't truly need every day for a week. If this seems too daunting, you could instead decide that you're going to give five articles of clothing to Goodwill or to another type of charity. Sometimes, when you decide that you're going to give your stuff to a better cause instead of simply throwing it away, the reality sets in that your stuff would maybe be more useful if it wasn't sitting idly in your house and was instead being used by someone who truly needs it more than you do.

Turn Daily Activities into Rituals

Lastly, being more indulgent in regards to yourself can also involve treating the daily things that you do in a way that is more ritualistic in nature. For example, instead of simply taking a shower on a weeknight, why not take the time to shower yourself in some indulgence and prepare for a bath instead? This bath could include the purchasing of candles, your favorite bottle of wine, and maybe even a good book or a playlist of your favorite soothing music. If you think baths are gross and you'd rather not take one, you can still pamper yourself in other ways. Purchasing a fancy foot cream or a face mask are two other types of treats in which you can indulge that will turn your typical evening into something that is just a little bit more special.

Additionally, it's important to note here that it is quite hygge to invest in spa days or spa treatments of any type. These types of treatments can range from getting a massage to going to the gym and spending a long period of time in the sauna or hot tub. These treatments, while often luxurious, can also often come with a price tag that is not desirable for some. If you're someone who would rather not spend a load of money on a spa treatment, you can always opt to take the spa treatment into your own hands. Giving yourself a manicure or even taking some time to think about how you can make your wardrobe more creative are both ways that you can spend some time pampering and improving the way that you feel and look.

CHAPTER 7

ACTIVITIES WITH FRIENDS THAT ARE SO HYGGE IT HURTS

While the previous chapter documented what you can do while you have alone time, it's safe to say that there can come a point when too much alone time is not a good thing. This chapter will talk about activities that you can perform with your friends that go beyond hosting a dinner party or having a game night at your house. We don't all live in a place where winter seems to be the season that is the most prevalent, but that doesn't mean that hygge ideals cannot be attainable. Let's take a look at some of the activities that you can do with others in both a friendship capacity as well as in a capacity that will help you to become more integrated in your community.

Go Camping

One of the best ways to engage and invest in the elements that surround you in life is to go camping with your friends. Once you're in the natural elements, there are plenty of activities that you can do that will make your time in nature seem both fulfilling and entertaining at the same time. For example, you can go hiking, fishing, and even take a stab at building your own campfire if you feel so inclined. It's important to note here that the advice to go camping does not imply that you should spend the majority of your time at the campsite drinking. Sure, drinking can be a fine activity to do with friends, but hygge is about experiencing life naturally, rather than through the lens of a drunken stupor.

Sweater Swap

Another great way that you can get more involved with your community and not just with the friends that you currently have is to initiate some sort of sweater swap in your community. Of course, if you live in a place that generally experiences a warmer climate throughout the year, a sweater swap may not be appropriate; however, you can always change the article of clothing in question so that it better fits with the season in which you're planning to do the swap. Additionally, if you're coordinating this activity, it would probably a good idea to ensure everyone that you are personally going to be washing the clothes so that everything is truly clean prior to the swap event. After everything is clean, you'll also want to expect each item of clothing in question to make sure that all of the clothing matches in terms of quality.

Consider Taking Up a New Group Hobby

Another way that you can spend more time with the people in your life is to take up a new hobby with them. For example, if you live in a place where there is a lot of beautiful nature, why not get a group together to go on weekly hikes with each other, or find a few people who will try a new sport workout activity with you. Along these same lines, it's important to understand that hygge involves thinking about exercising in general a bit differently than you may currently be used to doing. Instead of thinking about working out as an activity that will ultimately lead to great results for your body, hygge ideals advocate for exercise to be more leisure and less productive. For example, if you're going to the gym, why not simply do activities that make you feel good, rather than perform an activity simply because it will result in a physical benefit but is rather unpleasant to perform itself. The *process* of the sport should be as pleasurable as the results that will come from it.

Rent a Dog for the Day

If you do not currently own a dog, another option that you have that would be fun to do with friends is to rent a dog for a day. What is cozier than cuddling up with a dog in the park or on the beach? When you do this with other people, you're all able to share in the joy of hanging out with a cute and cuddly animal for at least a day or two. Plus, when you decide to partake in this type of activity with friends, you're also able to bring the cost of doing this down. On average, renting a dog on a weekend day is going to cost you around forty dollars for the day. On a weekday, borrowing a dog will only cost around twenty-five dollars, but it's more likely that you would be borrowing a dog on the weekend and not during the week.

If you already own a dog, you can still spend time with your dog and others all at the same time. Remember, hygge is all about showing the people in your life that you care about them. When you own a pet, you can also extend this notion to your animal. Your animal needs just as much, if not more, recognition of the fact that you love them on a frequent basis. Additionally, bringing your dog or other type of pet around people who you trust and care about can be an enjoyable thing for both the animal and friends who are involved.

Go Ice Skating

This next activity is pretty winter-like in nature, for the simple fact that you're not going to be able to go ice skating if you live in a place where all of the ice is going to melt. Ice skating is considered to be a hygge activity for a few different reasons. Firstly, you have to dress in a cozy way when you ice skate so that you don't freeze while you're on the ice. Secondly, ice skating often brings with it warm drinks such as hot cocoa or coffee, which are also hygge-like drinks. Lastly, ice skating is an activity that is both active and enjoyable at the same time (unless you're someone who falls on the ice more than you skate on the ice). If you live in a place where it's often warm instead of chilly, you can still plan to partake in winter sports. Planning a ski trip with friends can be an incredibly fun and memorable time.

Take Up Yoga

These days, it seems like yoga is everywhere. If you're currently someone who is weirded out by the thought of doing strange poses in yoga pants or loose shorts, hear me out. Yoga often goes hand-in-hand with meditation, and can offer you a great way to turn inward and find out more about yourself than you could probably ever imagine. While yoga is largely an individual activity, it's an activity that can be done with friends at the same time. If you've never tried yoga before, then grabbing a few friends and heading to a yoga studio will likely relax some of the tension or apprehension that you may feel surrounding the activity. If yoga is something that you're willing to try with some friends, it's incredibly important that you take some time to think about the type of yoga that you want to do. As was already stated, yoga seems to be everywhere today. This means that there are many different types of yoga that's out there. Are you someone who would prefer a gentle yoga class, a class for true beginners, or an intense class that is more like a workout class in nature? If you don't choose the class that best fits your personality and individual style, you'll likely walk away from the experience feeling frustrated or bad about yourself.

CHAPTER 8

HYGGE FASHION TIPS THAT WILL MAKE YOUR WARDROBE POP

Now that we've discussed many activities that you can do both by yourself and with friends, this final chapter is going to discuss how you can dress yourself while you're doing these activities that are aligned with hygge principles. After you're finished reading this chapter, you should be able to combine all of the tactics that were presented in this book and begin to live by hygge ideals in a way that will lead to a comfier and most importantly happier way of life. Let's take a look at some of the hygge fashion rules that you can live by, so that your wardrobe can start to match your overall demeanor and attitude towards life in general.

Function Over Fashion

The single most important hygge wardrobe principle involves thinking about fashion in a way that is primarily practical. This largely has to do with matching your wardrobe with the type of environment in which you find yourself during any given event or point in time. For example, if you've ever been to college in a location where the climate is cold, then you know that there are many girls who choose to go out on the weekends in skimpy dresses and short skirts in the freezing cold without a jacket or a coat on. These girls are not in any way shape or form living with hygge in mind. If these girls were to adhere to hygge ideals, it would mean that instead of wearing these dresses and skirts that are barely there, they'd be wearing heavy clothing that leaves them feeling comfy and cozy. Even if you don't remember any of the other rules that were presented in this chapter, the notion of function over fashion is inherent to the entire hygge fashion culture. Of course, this doesn't mean that you have to walk around looking frumpy or ugly, but if an individual were put into a situation where he or she had to choose between being cold in a pretty spaghetti-strap dress or being warm in a wool dress that looked like a potato sack, a true hygge enthusiast would choose the potato sack every time.

Think More Layers

In addition to thinking about how clothing can serve a function rather than be completely cute or pretty, another crucial aspect to understanding hygge fashion is the idea of layering your clothing as well. For example, if it's cold outside, why not consider wearing a pair of leggings or long underwear underneath the pants that you're going to wear to work? If you take the time to really think about what's going to look good from a layering perspective, there's no reason why your layering techniques can't be both cute and warm all at the same time.

Knits Are In

Because so much of hygge revolves around being warm when it's cold outside, another significant trend that has emerged in terms of hygge style has to do with knits. Let's go back to our example of the scantily-clad dressed college girl for a moment. Let's say that instead of choosing to wear a spaghetti strap dress when it is snowing outside with no jacket on, this person instead chooses to adorn herself in a dress that was entirely made of wool. This decision would be incredibly hygge in nature. Along with clothing that is entirely made of wool, another trend that's apparent within hygge fashion is fringe. The idea behind using both knits and fringe as staples of the hygge fashion movement could be because both of these types of fabric choices can be found on blankets, which are about as cozy as it gets.

Think Simple

As we've already discussed earlier in this book, an aspect of hygge involves living simply. This idea of simplicity also translates to hygge clothing, and most notably manifests itself with the color black. While an outfit that is entirely made of black clothing may seem goth or harrowing to come, an all-black outfit compliments the hygge fashion ideal quite nicely. If you're thinking about picking out an all-black outfit for yourself that exists within the hygge spectrum, you should be trying to keep in mind that the bulkier the top, the better. On the other hand, the bottoms for the outfit should be less bulky and snugger to the body.

If you completely disagree with the notion of dressing yourself in an entirely black outfit, you still have options. For example, you can still mix and match your tops and bottoms, but keep the contrast simple rather than stark. Patterned clothing should be worn to a minimum, unless you are contrasting the pattern with some type of bold and single color or design. Lastly, if you are someone who simply does not want to wear colors that are close in color or pattern, you can instead spice up your wardrobe with some kind of accessory piece or bag.

The Comfier the Socks, the Better

Another aspect of the hygge wardrobe that you're best not to do without are cozy and warm socks. Even if you're wearing a shoe that will not fit a sock that is particularly thick, you can still invest in a thin sock that will keep your foot adequately warm. These types of socks are called Merino socks. While they're not quite as warm as socks that are made of 100% wool, they're close to being as warm. Additionally, these socks are going to be able to fit into any type of boot that you're wearing, even if the boot is rather snug to your feet.

Earmuffs and Scarves

In keeping with the notion that your clothing should be functional before it's fashionable, two other essential items to have in your hygge closet are earmuffs and scarves. These days, you can easily find both earmuffs and scarves that are going to be able to match with the rest of your outfit. For scarves in particular, you should be able to also find one that will complement every season imaginable. People wear scarves in all types of climates, and the material of the scarf is going to be able to dictate how warm or how cool it will be for your neck. Earmuffs largely work in a similar manner. When it's only slightly chilly outside, fluffy earmuffs should be able to keep your ears adequately warm. On the other hand, if you're in a location where the weather is extremely cold and frigid, a hat or earmuffs that are lined with fleece may prove to be more appropriate.

CONCLUSION

Thank for making it through to the end of *Hygge: An Introduction to the Danish Art of Cozy Living*. Hopefully, this book has been able to serve as a source of comprehensive information regarding what the hygge lifestyle is and how it can benefit your life. Remember, you can use the information that was presented in this book to any extent that you'd like. The entire point of hygge is to use the tactics that exist within it in a way that will enhance the pleasure that you have in your life. By creating a cozy atmosphere for yourself and cultivating trust and enjoyment with the people around you, you'll be able to maximize the enjoyment that you can get out of your life, both over the short as well as the long-term.

The next step is to start integrating more hygge concepts into your life. The best idea here would be to choose the most appealing aspect of the hygge lifestyle that was presented in this book, and then work towards establishing these types of principles into your own life. It's important that while you're attempting to integrate these changes into your life that you take it at your own pace. If you move too quickly, there is always the chance that you will become overwhelmed, especially if the changes that you're looking to make are drastic. For example, if you're someone who has lived a life that is for the most part the complete opposite of hygge, then implementing a lot of hygge principles at once may ultimately make you feel overwhelmed. The best advice here is to take your time, and find pleasure in the act of changing your lifestyle tactics. This way, you're less likely to feel stressed or feel like hygge just isn't for you. Hygge is for everyone!

Finally, if you found this book useful in any way, a review on Amazon is always appreciated!

Made in United States
North Haven, CT
01 May 2023

36121220R00046